C000165646

BE MORE

Dolly

BE MORE

Dolly

----------☆----------

LIFE LESSONS
BEYOND THE
9 TO 5

HarperCollins*Publishers*

HarperCollins*Publishers*
1 London Bridge Street
London SE1 9GF

www.harpercollins.co.uk

First published by HarperCollins*Publishers* 2020

10 9 8 7 6 5 4 3 2 1

A catalogue record of this book is available from the British Library

HB ISBN 978-0-00-838376-3
EB ISBN 978-0-00-838377-0

Printed and bound by PNB, Latvia

MIX
Paper from
responsible sources
FSC™ C007454

FSC
www.fsc.org

This book is produced from independently certified FSC™ paper
to ensure responsible forest management.

For more information visit: www.harpercollins.co.uk/green

This work has not been officially endorsed by Dolly Parton, but is a homage to the great and wonderful Dolly. It is written by fans, for fans, and is a lasting tribute to her and everybody she inspires.

Thank you, Dolly.

CONTENTS

THE 10 DOLLY-MANDMENTS

1. *Thou shalt* wear what thou likest and feel comfortable in.

2. *Thou shalt* forgive but not be a doormat.

3. *Thou shalt* express thyself creatively to free thine inner queen.

4. *Thou shalt* be hardworking but still have a social life.

5. *Thou shalt* spread joy where thou can.

6. *Thou shalt* accept others for who they are.

7. *Thou shalt* help others with what means thou has.

8. *Thou shalt* stay true to thyself.

9. *Thou shalt* love thyself and love thy neighbour.

10. *Thou shalt* be thy badass self.

And to Begin Our Journey ...

A Love Letter to Dolly

Don't you just wish there was a little more Dolly in everyone? From the driver who cut you up on your way to the dentist to the colleague who puts the milk back in the fridge when there isn't enough left for one more cup of tea (there's a special place in hell for those people), to the bad bosses you've had or still have, to the world leaders and big decision-makers of our time ... If they had just a little bit of Dolly's joy for life, her hardworking tenacity, her acceptance of others, her creative spark and electrifying warmth, wouldn't the world be a better place?

'But how do I become more like Dolly?' we hear you ask ... Well, you're in the right place, because this is your ultimate guide to living like and just boldly *being* like Queen Dolly herself.

But what does this guide contain? Here, we share Dolly's whip-smart humour and gigantic pearls of wisdom, and help you to understand how *being* like Dolly and trying to live more like her is actually good for you, and for the world. We'll look at her razor-sharp business acumen, how she is always unapologetically herself, how she loves her community and always gives back when she can, her advice on love and heartache and how she can teach us to be our best selves. We'll also throw in some fun quizzes, games and activities along the way!

Now, let's begin with something rather beautiful: a love letter to the lady herself. She has brought so much love to us, let's start by giving some back.

Dear Dolly,

Thank you.

Thank you for bringing such heartfelt, raw, honest music into our lives. But thank you also for not taking yourself too seriously, because there's nothing worse than a successful person who can't laugh at themselves. Thank you for showing that you can look how you want, dress how you want, and still get to where you want to be without having to sacrifice who you are. Thank you for being you. Thank you for your unbridled positive attitude. We know you might not feel like being that way every day, but thank you for sharing that part of yourself with us.

Thank you for the wigs – we want more. Thank you for the rhinestones – there are never too many. Thank you for the jokes – keep 'em coming. Thank you for your generosity – the world is definitely a better place because you have power in it. And on that subject, thank you for using your power for good.

Thank you for creating the world's best-named theme park – it brings us joy whenever we think about it. Thank you for teaching us it's OK to have desires and to go through heartache. Thank you for teaching us it's OK to be human. Thank you for encouraging us to embrace our individuality and differences, and to accept others as they are. Thank you for being there through every life change, on every road we've taken that didn't quite work out, for every success, for every fight and through grief, happiness and everything else in between.

Thank you for bearing it all through your music and for putting so many things into words that we find hard to say. Thank you for sharing your gift with us, and for making us feel as though we are part of it.

Thank you for loving dogs. Thank you for being the sister, auntie, mother, friend to us all at the same time. Thank you for being a light in what can be a very dark world at times, but before we get too serious, thank you for saying you'd invite Jennifer Aniston to a threesome – we all wanted to say that and now it's out there in the world.

Thank you for all your wisdom and the sass with which you deliver it. We're all better people for listening to you and having you in our lives.

All our love,
The World*

* (Yes, we've decided that everyone in the world wanted to write this letter and agrees with it.)

'When I got somethin' to say, I'll say it.'

Dolly

SAYS 'DO YOU'

I n the beginning, there was Dolly and her guitar ... At the tender age of 10, Dolly Parton picked up a guitar and found her true calling. As one of 12 children, she came from a very humble background, but that didn't stop her pursuing her passion with the great grit and zeal we have all come to love her for. The day after graduating from high school, she packed up her belongings and made the move from the small family home in the Tennessee Smoky Mountains to Nashville to pursue her music career. She knew that it would take a lot of work and determination, but young Dolly persisted. In 1970 – just six years after moving to Nashville – she had her first number-one single with 'Joshua' at the age of 24. Now, what can we learn from Dolly's drive to follow her passion against all the odds? Well, it has been scientifically proven that having a passion or purpose improves your health and increases your longevity.

Research carried out by explorer and author Dan Buettner, who studies the world's Blue Zones, where people live the longest, discovered that those who have a life purpose can live up to seven years longer! Buettner looked at what the longest-living people in the world had in common. He identified nine shared traits – and having a strong life purpose was one of them. The Japanese call this *ikigai*, which translates as 'Why I wake up in the morning'. Your personal *ikigai* needs to be:

'Find out
who you are
and do it on
purpose.'

- Something you love
- Something you are good at
- Something the world needs
- Something you can get paid for

And Dolly has hit every single one of these points (well, she's actually smashed them). She is definitely doing something she loves and something she is good at, and the world desperately needs what she is dishing out! Dolly is now in her seventies and shows no sign of slowing down. From beginning her career in the Sixties, to the recent release of her latest album for the soundtrack of the Netflix movie *Dumplin'* and the new musical 9 to 5 hitting the West End in London in 2019, with all music and lyrics written by Dolly, it is safe to say, she has longevity.

BE MORE DOLLY

Think about activities or hobbies you have a passion for. Are you taking the time to pursue them?

Put time in the diary this week to do something you love, for no other reason than you want to!

Dolly's songs are raw, honest and sometimes smack you right across the face and in the feels. This is what people love about her. They talk time and again about how her music resonates with them because it focuses on the *entire* human experience: love, loss, death, happiness, heartbreak, poverty, morality … the list is endless. Her unflinching honesty is something the world needs and it is undoubtedly one of the reasons for her phenomenal success. The 1975 song 'The Bargain Store' couldn't be more spot on about the messy ups and downs of a life lived fully. It may have been too honest for some, though, at the time of its release, as it was one of Dolly's songs that got banned from radio stations because of its 'suggestive' lyrics. Another song of hers to be banned was 'Touch Your Woman', as this was also seen as too graphic! But we think Dolly was just keeping it real; she said that she never thought of the lyrics of 'The Bargain Store' as a 'dirty thing'. Have a listen and see what you think!

When asked about the lyrics of 'The Bargain Store', Dolly simply said, 'I felt black and blue and I just wanted to heal back up and mend myself back together and get on with my life,' to which I think we can all say, 'Preach!' Dolly is unashamedly unafraid to speak her personal truth. And truth is what we all need right now. In a time when social media is king (or queen) and we're constantly bombarded with images of people's perfect filtered lives, Dolly's lyrics are a wonderful unfiltered antidote that won't make us compare ourselves to others but instead makes us feel a connection with this strong, badass, successful woman who admits that neither she nor her life is perfect.

'I know who I am, I know what I can do and can't do. I know what I will and won't do. I know what I am capable of and I don't agree to do things that I don't think I can pull off.'

Dolly is a great example of what sticking to your morals and values can achieve. She is smashing through that glass ceiling with her perfectly manicured nails whenever she can, being one of just seven female singers to win the Country Music Association's Entertainer of the Year award (in 1978). When she found out she had won, she reportedly said: 'I've built my own business and never had to do anything I didn't want to do.'

Dolly completely trusts her own instincts, which can be hard to do in a world with a deluge of conflicting information at your fingertips 24/7. As usual, Dolly is right! A recent article by Susanna Newsonen in *Psychology Today* states, 'Your intuition is shaped by your past experiences, and your existing knowledge which you gained from them.' Making you the best judge of what is right for you.

Following your intuition or gut instinct also naturally makes you act in line with your core values and maintain your credibility. Basically, your stomach knows best! Dolly has always been clear on what she thinks and what she believes in. She adapted to each era she has lived through, but her core values have stayed the same.

BE MORE DOLLY

Listen to your gut – it knows!

Write down three occasions when you have followed your gut
instinct and what happened. Got a tricky decision to make?
Use the space below to try to work out what
your gut is trying to tell you.

....

....

....

....

....

'You don't know how people are
looking at you. You just hope you
do well. You just come up with your
dreams and you dream 'em and
you pray and you work hard.'

It's no secret that Dolly has legions of fans among us mere mortals, but she has touched the hearts and minds of people across the music industry, too. The American country music singer, songwriter and record producer Maren Morris said, 'Just everything that she encapsulates has inspired me.' At the 2019 MusiCares charity gala, where Dolly won the Person of the Year award, Katy Perry, Miley Cyrus and Mark Ronson (to name a few) honoured Dolly by performing covers of her most famous songs. Seeing that women can make it to the top of their game with integrity demonstrates what is achievable. This is particularly important for young women in the spotlight. Knowing you can be who you want to be without needing to change your principles and morals is invaluable.

Dolly has said that she feels incredibly humbled to have had an influence on people and hasn't taken it for granted. She is basically an angel in human form.

Now, although we all know what Dolly thinks about the 9 to 5, she is hardly a routine and comfort kind of girl. But why is moving out of your comfort zone a positive thing?

According to an article in the *New York Times*, you need to find the perfect balance between being slightly out of your comfort zone to make you productive, but also not too far out of it, as that can make you unproductive, so what you need to experience is 'optimal anxiety'. Trying new things under your own steam (as opposed to being forced by circumstances) can make you more resilient to change – and if there is one thing that's certain in life, it's change!

Dolly has always been ready to move outside of her comfort zone. In 1973 she decided it was time to leave the machine that was musical variety TV hit *The Porter Wagoner Show*. This was an incredibly stressful time as it was the number-one syndicated show in country music and Porter was not particularly keen on letting his bright young star leave. Dolly and Porter had had huge hits together, but she knew it was time to strike out on her own. In order to convince Porter that it was the right thing for her to do, she just went home and wrote a little song you may have heard of, called 'I Will Always Love You'. And the rest is history ...

It has also been said that moving out of your comfort zone encourages creativity. The need for Dolly to think creatively about how she could break out and try new things encouraged her to write one of her best-known hits.

An article in *Forbes* magazine claims that creativity will be the most coveted skill of the future. Sure, technology is a pretty big deal, but creativity is the force behind all technological advancements. 'But I wasn't born creative,' we hear you whine! Well, that thinking is becoming a thing of the past! Elizabeth Gilbert, author of *Eat, Pray, Love* and *Big Magic*, believes that if you're alive then you're a creative person. You don't need permission to be creative and being creative shouldn't only be associated with art, music or dancing. You can be creative through problem-solving – it is just about using your imagination.

All you need to do is to ensure that you're creating space and making time for your creativity to flourish. Have a think about what you do when you're waiting for a train. What do you do when you're early for a date? How about when you're waiting for a coffee to brew? Let's take a guess ... You're looking at your phone, checking your emails or Instagram, replying to a friend on WhatsApp about which date in the diary none of you will ever be able to make ...

BE MORE DOLLY

Have a go at writing some Dolly-inspired lyrics on something you feel strongly about next time you're tempted to keep scrolling through social media.

Alternatively, draft an inspiring note to a friend who needs a little Dolly boost. Don't forget to add in some Dolly sparkle with her best quotes!

....

....

....

....

....

....

....

....

'MY SONGS ARE THE DOOR TO EVERY DREAM I'VE EVER HAD AND EVERY SUCCESS I'VE EVER ACHIEVED.'

This is a real phenomenon. We aren't used to doing nothing, and if our brains are constantly occupied, when does the good stuff happen? When do you get to think about what you would actually like to do this weekend? Or how you're going to solve problem X, Y or Z at work? Answer: you're not. Catherine Price, author of *How to Break Up with Your Phone*, created a 30-day plan to help people find their screen/life balance. An article in *Parade* magazine claims that using smartphones during our downtime is stopping us from being able to create connections and join the dots between different things, which, as we know, is basically creativity in its rawest form.

A really wonderful tip from Catherine on how to break this bad habit is to remember that you'll only experience and remember what you pay attention to. This means that when you decide what to pay attention to in the moment, you're making a broader decision about how you're spending your life. Deep, huh?!

Think about all the things Dolly is paying attention to: her music, her business, her charity work. By focusing on all of this, she is directing her energy towards what's important and is therefore creating the life she wants.

Songwriting and performing have built Dolly's whole life, but what are the perks of playing an instrument and listening to music for us mere mortals? Well, playing and practising music makes you so much more creative!

Having to perfect and practise something (effectively problem-solving) really helps wake up the creative side of the brain. However, that isn't the only benefit of learning to play an instrument; it also makes you smarter. This explains a *lot* about Dolly! Research has shown that learning to play an instrument makes you use both the left and right sides of your brain, which, in turn, enhances your memory. It also improves spatial reasoning and literacy skills.

Also, think about the dedication and discipline you need to learn an instrument. Well, Dolly can reportedly play eight: dulcimer, banjo, guitar, harmonica, piano, recorder, autoharp and saxophone. Phew, it's exhausting just listing them! She's also self-taught (but she's Dolly, so let's just appreciate how amazing she is rather than being jel!). Dolly is the *definition* of a grafter. You don't get to be at the top of your game in your seventies without some serious hard work.

Learning an instrument is not the only way to gain the above benefits, though; any type of lifelong learning is really good for you. Many of us still believe that once you leave school, college or university and get the job you have always wanted then that's it with learning – you're free! But, if you think about it, it might not have been the learning part that you didn't enjoy at school. It may have been the environment, or the forced deadlines and exams. However, if you could learn at your own pace and specialise in topics that really interest you or you have a passion for, just imagine what knowledge you could gain.

Having a passion outside of your day-to-day working life gives fresh meaning to your free time. You may not have the 'dream' job yet, but your daily grind may be helping to fund other passions outside of work. Learning about new topics or new skills gives you a great sense of achievement and may eventually lead to a job you want, or it could just bring you enjoyment. It is not always necessary to learn something for the sake of adding it to your CV or improving your career outlook. We often forget that we can try new things just for the fun of it. It might improve other aspects of your life,

too, and you may feel less resentful about working full-time if you know it is helping you to do more things you enjoy. You might make new friends, and who knows where they might lead you? Or you might just have more energy and enthusiasm for life! It'll encourage healthier habits, too, as you will need to get organised to create time to do this new hobby, and your newfound dedication and discipline may even spill over into other areas of your life.

As the old adage goes, 'If you want something done, give it to a busy person'. Learning a new skill doesn't have to take over your whole life, though. This is the biggest barrier for people wanting to change habits and learn new things. Even one to five minutes a day spent practising a new skill adds up over a few weeks, and you won't feel like you need to carve masses of time out of your already busy schedule to gain this skill. Small changes at a time will mean you are more likely to keep up this habit and adjust to a more positive mindset so you can believe you can accomplish new things. Think how proud you will be of yourself! Dolly would be proud, too!

If you'd rather belt out a tune than pick up an instrument then that's good news, too! An article in digital magazine *The Conversation* claims that singing has both physical and social benefits. Singing in a group or in a choir helps you form bonds with people very quickly. And the physical benefits include improved breathing and posture. The regulation and depth of the breath used for singing can help to relax the body, just as it does in yoga. Singing also has positive effects on our mental wellbeing. According to *The Conversation* magazine, research has shown that 'people feel more positive after actively singing than they do after passively listening to music or after chatting about positive life events'. No

wonder Dolly is so cheery all the time – she has been singing since she could talk!

Singing and music is such an innate and historic part of human culture. (The oldest musical instruments are thought to be over 40,000 years old. They are flutes carved from bird bone and mammoth ivory.) Even 40,000 years ago musical instruments were thought to have been used for recreational purposes, and, according to the BBC, music may have been a way for Homo sapiens to expand their wider social network. So come on, do as your great-great-great-great- (times a thousand maybe?!) grandparents did and make some sweet music to make some sweet connections.

Simply listening to music has major perks, too. It has the ability to reduce feelings of stress. Relaxing music can lower your heart rate, which, in turn, lowers your blood pressure. By lowering stress, it increases productivity and can support meditation, as it keeps the mind focused.

'I ain't never far away from a pen and paper or a tape recorder. I write every day, even when I'm on a plane, in the tub or on the bus. It burns in me. Songwriting is my way of channelling my feelings and my thoughts. Not just mine, but the things I say, the people I care about. My mind would explode if I didn't get some of that stuff out. Not everything I write is good, but it's all good for me – like therapy,' said Dolly in a *New York Times* interview in 2002.

And listening to Dolly is a type of therapy, right?! Can I get an amen? Amen!

However, we can also learn something from Dolly's daily writing habits. No, we don't need to be writing song lyrics, but we could be journalling as a way to get beneath our busy thoughts and try to understand our feelings. An article by Barton Goldsmith in *Psychology Today* claims that 'journalling is a tried and true way of tuning into your feelings and helping yourself make the changes that you desire'. You can simply write as and when you feel like it if that works for you, or the article also suggests having a go at 'gratitude journalling'. This involves writing down three to five different things you are grateful for each night. Within a few weeks of doing this, results have shown that people claim to feel much more positive about their lives.

Writing also brings you to the present moment and encourages mindfulness. It allows you to truly home in on what you are feeling and why. A surprising benefit of journalling is that it apparently boosts self-confidence. By writing about a positive experience, you are effectively reliving it, which releases endorphins and dopamine to lift your mood. Writing also helps you get all your thoughts out and gives you time to process them. We've all had days when we have received an email that has made our blood boil and we want to fire off a snippy response – well, how about you write out a response but then don't send it? Take a few minutes after you have written it to go back over it and see if it is the right response. You will most likely find that it is not and will more likely make the situation worse. But, having got the words out on a page or screen will help you to see them in a wider context, taking them out of your mind and therefore taking a lot of the heat out of the moment. Seeing the words written in black and white takes a lot of the power out of them. When they are just in your head, they feel so much more powerful because your voice is attached to them and you can't help but play them on a continuous loop and wind yourself up even more. Writing them out gives you that breathing space and time to pause. However, writing doesn't just have to be about getting your frustration out on the page; it could be a way of expressing something beautiful that you can't say out loud. Even just words that come to you when you think of someone or something that you love could be linked together to make a wonderful poem or song. Just remember, no one has to see your writing if you don't want them to. It could just be for you and then you can truly express yourself.

No wonder Dolly is so chipper all the time if she's writing and singing herself through the day!

Dolly admits that not everything she writes is good. But has that stopped her? No! Perfectionism is something that plagues many of us and stops us finishing projects – or even, in most cases, starting them.

Professor Brené Brown describes perfectionism in her book *Daring Greatly* as 'believing that doing everything perfectly means you'll never feel shame'. In fact, perfectionism is not about personal growth or pushing for achievement and excellence; it is actually the belief 'that if we do things perfectly and look perfect, we can minimise or avoid the pain of blame, judgment and shame'.

But when do we get to be perfect? When will that project be perfect? When will your body be perfect? When will your relationships be perfect? Hmm … Never. Perfection doesn't exist. And if you are constantly striving for something that doesn't exist, you will never get there and you'll never feel a sense of achievement or satisfaction. Perfectionist thinking gives the appearance of control, but in reality, there is very little that is in your direct power. You can only try your best and give your best. If you are constantly terrified

of making an error and worrying about what people think of you, are you ever actually going to try the big stuff? The juicy, important stuff that you'll look back on and say, 'Hey, I did that'? Even if the thing you do or create doesn't turn out as good as you hoped, you can relax knowing that it was true to you at that time with the knowledge, resources, support and time you had. And that's an achievement you can be proud of. Over a lifetime you are going to make mistakes and there will be times when they feel like the worst things you have done in your life, but you will get five years down the line and you won't even remember what they are. If you are kind to yourself and kind to others then mistakes will just roll on by.

BE MORE DOLLY

☆

When was the last time you tried something new? Make a list opposite of new things you could do to gently nudge yourself out of your comfort zone. Remember, it's only a small step you need. Maybe get yourself to that yoga class you've wanted to go to for ages or take yourself out for lunch. Imagine the sense of accomplishment you'll feel afterwards.

☆

Do you need a phone break? Don't worry, we're not saying that precious smartphone of yours needs to go into permanent hibernation; maybe just think about those times of the day when you could be staring into space instead of staring at a screen. You never know, you might just solve that problem that's been niggling you for weeks.

☆

Flex that brain muscle! If you don't feel so inclined to learn an instrument, there are plenty of other ways to get that brain working. Read something completely new, try some brain-training apps – basically, try to surprise that big old brain of yours with new information or a new task, and you might be surprised by its reaction!

```
    .............................................................................

    .............................................................................

    .............................................................................

    .............................................................................

    .............................................................................
```

Dolly said in an interview in *Forbes* magazine in 2012 that 'I don't believe there are that many mistakes in this world. I think everything's a stepping stone and even if you make what is a so-called mistake in somebody else's eyes, to me, it's something you learn from!'

Making mistakes is actually good for us. If we're not afraid to make mistakes, it encourages us to try new things and, as Alina Tugend, author of *Better by Mistake: The Unexpected Benefits of Being Wrong*, says, we should focus on the process and effort rather than the results, because when we fear error, we miss out on some of the most fun and exciting things in life. Mistakes are also so important in teaching resilience. If you have never failed at anything, when the time actually comes for you to fail (trust us, it comes to us all) it's going to feel like the world is ending and you'll have no coping strategies for dealing with it. Coming back from that will be hella hard. However, if you have learnt that messing up is not the end of civilisation as you know it, you'll be bouncing back in no time. Owning your mistakes gives the power back to you. There is no need to rake over the mistake and make yourself feel bad or guilty, but trying to see where and why you went wrong can be helpful in learning what to do differently next time. After all, it's not about the mistake you made, it's about how you reacted and recovered from it that counts. As another badass woman, Sophia Loren, said: 'Mistakes are part of the dues one pays for a full life.'

BE MORE DOLLY

☆

Next time you're feeling a bit overwhelmed, try listening to some relaxing music to distract your brain.

☆

Have a go at a gratitude journal. Set yourself the goal of doing it for one week and see how you feel afterwards. Remember, it only has to be three to five different things a day that you're grateful for. Just make sure they are different things each day!

☆

Remember, everybody makes mistakes. They are actually good for you, as they give you a chance to learn and grow.

How to 'Do You' the Dolly way:

- Do what you love as much as you can. Make time in your diary – it's important!
- Write yourself some inspiring lyrics and be as straight-talking as you can. Speak your truth!
- Listen to your gut!
- Maybe grab some pictures of people who inspire you (it doesn't have to be just Dolly) and stick them around your mirror so you can see them every day.

'I've done business with men who think I'm as silly as I look. By the time they realise I'm not, I've got the money and gone.'

Dolly

MEANS
BUSINESS

Does the thought of talking about money make you cringe and blush? Well, you are not alone. A recent study by Fidelity Investments of over 1,500 women revealed that 80 per cent of the participants did not like talking to people close to them about money. A major factor holding women back was confidence, and not knowing who to turn to for advice.

Dolly, however, knows her value and knows money is no shame-trigger – it is damn right important to talk about it! From the beginning of her career, Dolly knew that music was a business and she would need to take the lead on what was right for her and her money (a.k.a. her #DollyDollar).

Her dad, Robert, was a big inspiration for this, stating, 'Don't let other people take advantage of you. Keep your mind on your business.' And this has stood her in pretty good stead in those killer heels of hers, as she was named number 71 on the *Forbes* Celebrity 100 list for the first time in her career at the age of 71! She had a 63-date tour in 2017, which contributed to this success, as well as a hefty income from her (incredible) theme park, Dollywood.

Dolly is the definition of having many fingers in many pies: she has her own publishing company for the rights to her songs; she owns her own theme park; she writes lyrics for film and theatre; she tours endlessly, acts in movies and owns Sandollar Productions, a media company that is responsible for the eight-part mini-series on Netflix called *Heartache*, based on Dolly's songs. She is also planning to team up with IMG on a licensing deal to create clothing, homeware and many other products her avid fans are sure to love. On top of all this, she also makes time for her charity work, which includes the Imagination Library – a fantastic initiative devoted to inspiring a love of reading in the hearts and minds of children across the US, UK, Australia and Canada, to name a few.

An article in the *Harvard Business Review* from 2017 states that having more than one career leaves you feeling happier and more fulfilled. The benefits are pretty clear, including: making new friends from different walks of life, interdisciplinary thinking and using your day job to fund the development of new skills or hobbies you have a real passion for. Dolly has explored many creative avenues to help her lead a rewarding life. She never takes monetary success for granted, though, saying in a 2017 BBC interview, 'As soon as you start making money, you should invest and get into other businesses that you can fall back on if you don't make it big, or if you make it big and you fall on hard times.'

The study by Fidelity Investments of women and money showed that 75 per cent of women want to learn more about investing, but only 47 per cent of the women surveyed would feel happy talking to a professional about investing on their own. Maybe if we could adopt the Dolly confidence and embrace talking about the #DollyDollar, that percentage could increase and female investors could come to the fore! Dolly is not afraid to show her ambition and desire to earn money, and neither should we be.

Not long after Dolly released her classic ballad 'I Will Always Love You' in 1974, the king of rock 'n' roll himself, Elvis Presley, requested to cover it. Do you know what Dolly said in response? She said, 'No.' Well, maybe not as bluntly as that, but she did stick to her daddy's advice and passed on this deal, as it would have meant relinquishing *half* of the publishing rights – and Dolly does not do things by halves. Can you imagine people's reaction to this at the time?! It would have been many artists' ultimate dream to have Elvis cover their song, but Dolly knew she had to follow her father's advice and not let *anyone* take advantage of her.

'Well, it was just one of those first really hard business decisions I had to make.'

So, did this risky decision pay off? You can bet your rhinestoned bottom it did. Whitney Houston's 1992 cover for the film *The Bodyguard* went platinum in many countries around the world. Contrary to the deal offered by Elvis's manager, Dolly received a hefty sum for the publishing and writing of the song, as well as a royalty for Whitney's version. It is believed that this song alone has made Dolly $20 million (or 20 million Dolly Dollars, we should say), and this would not have been possible had she gone against her gut instinct.

An article in *Forbes* states that small businesses and entrepreneurs should not allow their current urgency for cash to override their consideration of the future of their business. Cash should not be king over salient business decisions and how they may affect customers. Dolly could have easily agreed to allow Elvis half the publishing rights and it would have probably been one of the most successful songs of that era, but it would have gone against her business model and ultimately set a precedent that could have slowly hip-thrusted (tenuous metaphor, we know) away her business empire. The respect this decision garnered among her peers firmly cemented her as a businesswoman who couldn't be swayed easily, and it laid the groundwork for all future business deals. Dolly knows life and business are marathons, not sprints.

BE MORE DOLLY

Do you stick to your guns in business or life decisions, or are you easily swayed? Journal below about the last difficult decision you made and what factors influenced your final choice. Was it fear, money or pressure from external factors? How could you change this next time so that your decisions align with your beliefs?

Never feel pressured to make quick decisions. Take your time, listen to some Dolly songs to help strengthen your resolve. The song '9 to 5' is great for when you want to get riled up about fighting the system! You go, Dolly lover!

....

....

....

....

....

In Dolly's commencement address to the University of Tennessee graduates of 2009 she talked about the great passion she has for what she does. Do you think she could have kept going for all these years in one of the most gruelling and competitive industries without a huge drive and passion? She told them a beautiful story of how, when she was a young girl, she would fit a tin can onto a broom handle and use it as a microphone. She would pretend that the chickens in the yard were her audience as she strummed away at her guitar. Now, many of us have these ideas as children and these tend to fade away as we move into the 'real' world. However, Dolly says there is a big difference between dreams and wishes. Dreams are when you visualise yourself achieving what is really important for you, which will drive you forward to work hard to get there, whereas wishes are mere hopes with no conviction or work behind them. So first off, you have to make sure that what you want are dreams and not wishes. One step on from Dolly's role-playing and visualising is the technique known as a vision board.

A vision board can be used to try to map out your goals and dreams visually using pictures and words so they are clearer in your mind. According to psychologist Barbara Nussbaum in an article in *Forbes*, vision boards are so effective because the sensory experience of creating one allows us to emotionally connect with our dreams and goals. And when we emotionally connect with something, we are more invested in it. We do need to make sure that the vision boards are as detailed as possible, though, otherwise they won't be as effective. The more detail they have, the more we connect and invest in them. It takes the idea from being a wish to a dream that you can see yourself achieving. Creating a physical board will also turn that idea from just something you 'want' to something you could realistically have. Place the board somewhere you can see it every day and it will be a happy reminder of why you are doing what you are doing.

If you don't fancy making a vision board, you can go straight to visualisation. This is something elite athletes have done for a long time, running through the motions of scoring a goal or finishing a race in a certain time. They have already practised different eventualities and how they will react when they come up in real life. Imagine yourself completing your dream/goal. How will you feel when you have done this? Who is there? What will your body feel like? You can also visualise the steps to this goal. If it's writing a book, for example, you might imagine yourself researching in the library, taking notes and talking to friends about the idea. Again, think about how you feel at each stage: where are you? Who is with you? The more detail the better, so that it embeds in the brain.

Dolly didn't get to where she is by accident. It's great to be inspired and have dreams, but what's the difference between someone who is a dreamer and someone who is successful in their chosen field? Well, that's action. No one is going to hand you your goals on a plate, as ultimately, they are too busy thinking about what they are trying to achieve. You need to take steps towards each change and progression in your life by yourself.

A common fear people have is something called 'imposter syndrome'. This is where you don't feel like you deserve the role or opportunity you have been given and that sooner or later you are going to be 'found out'. You imagine your employers realising that you don't know what you are doing and saying that they've made a terrible mistake in hiring you. It can also mean that you never allow yourself to feel ready to take that leap to start a new project or job, because you don't feel you are qualified and you worry that people will discover your secret and 'out' you. This can lead to a lot of anxiety and will ultimately stop you from pushing yourself to try new things. Imposter syndrome is *very* common, especially when you are new to a role and feel like you have to prove yourself. Dolly would have been one of *thousands* of young people trying to make it in Nashville in the 1960s, and originally, not *everyone* was a fan of her singing style. She also encountered a lot of negativity when she first joined *The Porter Wagoner Show*, as she took over from a very popular female singer called Norma Jean. As we know, some people are not always a fan of change! If Dolly hadn't had her dreams/goals/missions (whatever you want to call them) to lend her inner strength, all of this negativity could have made her feel out of place or caused her to start believing that she was just a faker waiting for someone to take her out. Nonetheless, she persisted. She did so because she knew that nobody goes through life without negativity, animosity and criticism. No one gets a free ride. It's how you shape that criticism and disappointment, and whether you use it to drive yourself forward or hold yourself back. We all know how Dolly uses it. So have a think about how much time you spend ruminating on negative thoughts, on mistakes you have made in the past or what other people might think of you, or whether you belong somewhere, and think instead about how you could turn this around and make that negative picture a positive one.

The brain is naturally wired to pick up negative news or to think negatively. According to *Psychology Today*, neurological studies have shown that our brains light up more when encountering negative imagery as opposed to positive imagery. This is due to evolutionary factors. It makes sense that negative things register more strongly in the brain, as one of its primary functions is to keep us safe. The brain is wired to notice danger in the hope that you will take action against it, either by removing the threat or getting away from it. This bias in the brain makes modern life more difficult; with the barrage of information we receive daily, our brains are actively choosing to focus on the negative. The study goes on to say that in the modern world, you need five positive things to happen to outweigh one negative thing. It is a war of attrition against negative thoughts!

Imagine how much more energy you would have at your disposal if you spent that time thinking, 'Wow, what a great job I did today on that project,' or 'It's great that Susan likes my proposal,' (we all know a Susan at work) or 'I'm so pleased I got selected for that job, I worked really hard on that.' If you think about it, aren't these examples of how you would talk to your best friend? Isn't this how you imagine Dolly would talk to you? Encouraging, comforting, warm and loving. A good test of whether you should be thinking certain thoughts about yourself is to ask, 'Would I say this to my best friend?' and if your answer is 'Gosh, no!' then question why you are saying it to yourself! If the voice you hear most often is the one in your head (which, let's be honest, it is, as wherever you go, there you are) and that little voice is saying, 'You're not good enough for this, you're not good enough for that,' then who are you going to listen to? And is that little voice ever right? We know we can easily convince ourselves that a situation or circumstance is a certain

way, only to have that turned on its head when we get a different perspective. Imagine if you could get a different perspective on the thoughts going on in your head. Well, you can.

Writing your thoughts down can help you to get them out, sort through them and see how positively (or otherwise) you talk about yourself. You can then take action to change this if you need to. A great way to do this is to write down one thing every night that you are proud of doing that day. Write it on a piece of paper, then add this to a jar. Keep the jar by your bed and whenever you are feeling a bit down or demotivated, take out any of these notes and read them back to yourself as a reminder that you can be proud of what you have achieved and that you do regularly achieve things.

Dolly talks a lot about her practice of praying. She prays about things to find out what she should do. You might not feel comfortable with praying, but what if we just called it meditation? Learning how to meditate can have a hugely positive influence on your life. It is not learning how to stop thoughts, it is learning how to recognise what you are thinking, rather than it just being a constant unchecked process. You can then learn how to let those thoughts go. If you often find yourself dwelling on a thought or feel your thoughts spiralling, you can apply tricks to get your brain out of those habits. Meditation teaches you that your thoughts are *not* facts and that they actually have little bearing on what is happening. It essentially teaches you that thoughts and emotions are only ever temporary. What you feel now and how you are going to feel in an hour, a week or a month can be dramatically different. This gives you a greater sense of control and hope. If you can separate what your thoughts are telling you about how you feel and what's actually happening, and then take that moment to just step back and observe, you will be able to make much clearer decisions without the emotional baggage. You can step back and see how you really talk to yourself on a daily basis, as you probably don't even notice it. The only way Dolly got the (male-dominated) music industry in 1960s Nashville to sit up and take notice of her was by believing in herself, and you can't believe in yourself if you're talking trash about yourself every darn day.

Dolly has also spoken about how, on the day of her high-school graduation, each student had to say what they were going to do next. A young Dolly stood up and said she was going to Nashville to be a music star, and her words were greeted with laughter and sniggering from her fellow classmates. Dolly recalls wondering why they were laughing when that really was what she was going to do. Wouldn't it be amazing to have so much faith in yourself and your talents that you would immediately question why somebody would laugh at you, rather than take it as a criticism and make you question your plans? As Dolly says, 'Who is laughing now?' This is a lesson to us all about treating people's dreams and goals with respect. A lot of the time this kind of negative behaviour is triggered by jealousy of another's talent, but also jealousy that another person has a dream and such a strong belief in themselves that they will make their dream come true. It's also jealousy that this person believes they *deserve* big things to happen to them, as some people can't even begin to imagine that for themselves. If everyone treated themselves kindly and believed they deserved to have their needs met, there would be no need for laughing or jeering at other people's dreams.

BE MORE DOLLY

Grab some magazines and create yourself a beautiful vision board. Not only is this good for helping you visualise the outcome of your goals and dreams, but crafting is also a very mindful and creative process.

Start a 'Proud of Myself' jar! Note down on small scraps of paper what you've done that you're proud of and pop them into the jar. Another nice thing to do with this is to keep the jar sealed until New Year's Eve and then open and review the notes before starting the New Year. This will ensure you head into January with a positive mentality (and only a *slight* hangover).

Maybe consider downloading a meditation app and trying it for a short amount of time every day. Little and often is the key to meditation when you first start as it can feel very daunting sitting with your thoughts with little or no distraction. Guided meditations are best for beginners, as silence can feel very loud and helpful prompts by the practitioner will keep you on track.

Don't be scared of wanting to achieve something. Having a dream is scary, as it triggers anxiety over what will happen if you don't achieve it. Well, it turns out that nothing bad will happen, it'll just be a different life. It might even be a better one! The bigger fear should be not trying at all. So just try your best and enjoy the journey!

How to do business the Dolly way:

- Educate yourself about money. It is not an embarrassing topic – everyone needs it and the more you know about it, the better. You will feel more in control and able to make educated decisions about how to use it or save it.

- Is there a goal or milestone you would like to achieve? Do you believe you can achieve it? If not, how can you expect anyone else to believe that you will? Grab that Dolly spirit and solidify that goal in your mind or through a vision board. Seeing really is believing!

- Talk to yourself kindly. Imagine you are talking to your dearest friend in the world. You want them to feel love and encouragement and you need to feel that from yourself, too.

- Treat your own dreams and those of other people with respect. They are important and vital for everyone to have, and you don't know how much you will upset someone by not supporting them.

'I just think everybody should be loved and accepted for exactly who and what they are, and we should love ourselves exactly for who and how we are.'

Dolly

KNOWS EVERYONE
COUNTS

We all know the breadth of people who love Dolly: young, old, straight, LGBTQ+ – the list goes on. But why does she appeal to the hearts of so many? Well, we think it's because she understands what it feels like to be judged, but she continues to strive forward and embraces everyone, even those who might have misjudged her. She has famously been mocked and criticised for her sense of style, but as Dolly herself says:

'A lot of people have said I'd have probably done better in my career if I hadn't looked so cheap and gaudy. But I dress to be comfortable for me, and you shouldn't be blamed because you want to look pretty.'

It's hard enough to be yourself in day-to-day life as a 'non-celeb', so can you imagine what it must be like for Dolly to cling to her truth after living in the superficial world of celebdom for nearly six decades!

What sets Dolly apart from a lot of us is that she has never tried to fit in. She believes that she belongs anywhere and everywhere she wants to be. Brené Brown, researcher and storyteller, says in her book *The Gifts of Imperfection*, 'Fitting in is about assessing a situation and becoming who you need to be to be accepted. Belonging, on the other hand, doesn't require us to change who we are; it requires us to be who we are.' And who else personifies this more than Dolly? The courage to live as you want to in a world that is constantly telling you to be something else is powerful. Brené calls living to fit in 'soul-sucking', and we all know that feeling, don't we? It takes up so much precious energy to pretend to be something or someone we are not, and we could be using that energy to do what we really want to. Dolly doesn't seem to be wasting any of her magical energy on fitting in, and look what incredible things she has achieved with it!

Self-acceptance is a huge part of letting yourself just belong, rather than fit in. As Brené says, self-acceptance is believing that you are enough and that you are already worthy without 'achievements' or anything else to your name. And Dolly seems to have cracked this self-acceptance malarkey. In an interview with the *Guardian* in early 2019, when asked if she gets tired of being 'Dolly Parton', Dolly explained that she enjoys what she does: 'I look fake, but my world is real to me.' So long as Dolly knows in her own mind that she is real and authentic, ultimately it doesn't matter what other people think of her.

Over the years, Dolly has set some very clear boundaries to protect her privacy, which should also be an inspiration to us fans. In this age of social media, people are always trying to grab themselves a little more of the celebrity they admire, and often feel that they *deserve* to know the whole person (no-make-up selfie and all). As Brené Brown said in an article on Oprah.com, 'Daring to set boundaries is about having the courage to love ourselves, even when we risk disappointing others.' Dolly is not going to sacrifice herself just to please everyone else. As she has stated, 'Even though I'm public there's still a very private side. But that's what keeps me sane, and I guess it's what keeps people intrigued: they think they're going to find out something more. But you're only going to know as much as I'm going to tell you.'

Dolly isn't cheating us out of anything by not telling us every little detail about herself. She knows what she needs to do to keep herself happy and healthy, so she can be the best person for everyone. Boundaries are important for everybody to have in any relationship, at work or at home. Having clear boundaries means that we all understand what is expected of us, avoiding any confusion. They show that you have self-respect, and that you respect the time of the other person. If somebody tries to push your boundaries, you should carefully push back to reaffirm your position. At first, it will seem scary and difficult to tell people exactly what you would or wouldn't like, but eventually they will start to see that you are a person who knows their own mind, and they will respect that.

BE MORE DOLLY

Which hobby or activity would you take up if you weren't worried about what others might think of you? Do it! Reverse the soul-sucking!

Do you have clear boundaries both at work and in your personal relationships? Remember, it is kinder to yourself and to others if you are clear from the start about what you want. Dolly has the courage to be clear on her boundaries – you can, too.

Remember, you are worthy!

So, Dolly knows herself, she accepts herself and doesn't try to fit in, but she also sets clear boundaries to keep herself happy. This healthy attitude towards herself ensures that she can then have a healthy attitude towards everybody else, too. She creates the space to love herself, and therefore has the capacity to love others. Over the past three decades she has openly supported the LGBTQ+ community. Her Oscar-nominated song 'Travelin' Thru', written for the soundtrack of the 2005 film *Transamerica* about a pre-operative transgender woman, apparently earned her hate mail at the time. For a country icon who has legions of very conservative fans, it was a courageous stance for Dolly to take. She has been criticised in the past for not making public political statements and has been accused of doing this deliberately so as not to offend her fanbase, but in fact, she has been advocating for equality through her work for many years.

Dollywood, Dolly's theme park in the Sevier County where she grew up, has been described as being 'a safe haven in the rural South' for gay people. In the mid-2000s, 'Gay Day' was established at Dollywood. Even though it wasn't officially endorsed by Dolly, its existence showed that gay fans felt particularly comfortable there. When asked in an interview with the *New York Times* what kind of families were welcome at Dollywood's new DreamMore Resort, which opened in 2015 with rooms specifically designed for different-sized families, Dolly stated: 'A family is a family, whether you're a gay family or a straight family. If that's your family, you should be treated with the utmost respect, and we do that no matter what. I say a good Christian wouldn't be judging anyway. We're supposed to love and accept each other.' To have the founder of the biggest employer in Sevier County state that all families are welcome and accepted is a massive step in the right direction for such a typically conservative area. The song 'Family' is the perfect example of Dolly advocating acceptance and equality and embracing families, no matter their background.

An article in *Psychology Today* states that by accepting others as they truly are, you can find calm and peace within yourself. Dolly knows that acceptance is a wonderful gift to give and receive.

Dolly's extensive charity work is another testament to her inclusivity. Her belief that everyone – regardless of their background – deserves to have access to books, and her tireless pursuit to make

this happen, speaks volumes. Her relentless positivity is a gift to us all. The fact that Dolly can bring people together across the political, social and economic divides is proof of her innate power. It is no surprise that the crowd at a Dolly concert is one of the most diverse of any musical event. Her never-ending zest for life, her overwhelming talent, her emotive and unique voice, her poignant lyrics and her positive energy shine through to create a social glue that holds all these diverse groups of people together. When you're not scared of being the real you, you stop resenting yourself for pretending to be somebody else. This makes it so much easier to treat people the same way. Whipping up fear of others to unite a group only works for so long, as it is not built on a solid foundation, whereas uniting people through joy, love and connection lasts a lifetime. Dolly's ability to connect with people and connect people across the social divides is so powerful. Her songs from the early part of her career are timeless and mean as much now as they did when first written, because she gets to the core of the human condition. Some of her songs were progressive for their time, giving a voice to those who might not have traditionally had their say. She hasn't shied away from tough topics, such as suicide, and discusses them with such empathy and care that you can see why she has connected people across generations and across the world. There is a lot of comfort in knowing that over 50 years ago, somebody was going through the same things you are now, and they have made it through.

BE MORE DOLLY

Take time to think about what connects us rather than divides us. Someone you may never normally speak to might be a huge Dolly fan and they are someone worth getting to know.

Use the section at the back of the book called 'Dolly Tunes for the Soul' to get advice and comfort from Dolly when you need it, according to the situation.

Remember, people are all we have, so even if you find it hard to connect with someone, see if you can take the Dolly stance and just accept them for who they are.

How to be more inclusive the Dolly way:

- Remember, fitting in is not the same as belonging. Trying to fit in won't make you happy, so take some Dolly advice and be who you truly are.

- Having boundaries is important. Don't forget that it's fine if you don't want to tell someone something or don't want them to know something. There is still lots about Dolly that we don't know, and that's OK. She is her own person – she is allowed to have a private life, and we should respect that. Just because we have access to celebrities and online personalities 24/7 doesn't mean they owe us anything, and that goes for the people in our lives, too. Just because someone can text or email you at any time of the day or night doesn't mean you have to respond if you don't want to. A good way to handle the intrusive phone culture we have is to turn off all your notifications. That way, the phone doesn't control you, you decide when you want to look at it!

- Smiling at people doesn't cost you anything and might just brighten someone else's day. Go on, give it a try!

'I think everybody should be treated with respect. I don't judge people. I try not to get too caught up in all the controversy of things. I hope that everybody gets a chance to be who and what they are.'

'Being a star just means you find your own special place, and that you shine where you are.'

Dolly

KNOWS WHAT IT IS
TO BE AN ICON

'I'm not offended by the dumb blonde jokes because I know I'm not dumb. I also know I'm not blonde.'

Are you stumbling out of bed to pour yourself a cup of ambition every dang day? Then you know the 9-to-5 struggle is still real. The original 9 to 5 film was released in 1980 in a flourish of big hair and many a wonderful Jane Fonda pussy-bow blouse (if you know, you know), with a comedic-but-knowing look at women's roles in the workplace. Dolly plays the buxom blonde secretary to lecherous, sexist boss Franklin Hart Jr., and her character, Doralee Rhodes, becomes stuck between a rock and a hard place (or a bigot and the patriarchy) when she is being blackmailed into sleeping with her boss but knows she needs her job to support her family. She is at a loss as to how to say no to Franklin. Enter her sisters from another mister, Violet Newstead (played by Lily Tomlin) and Judy Bernly (pussy-bow-blouse Jane Fonda), who rally together in an attempt to off their boss.

You would hope that in this day and age, people wouldn't feel the need to try to murder their senior colleagues if extreme sexism was occurring in the workplace. A swift word with the HR team ought to put paid to the perpetrator's career. However, it's not quite so cut and dried in the film!

So, was *9 to 5* the pre-cursor to the #MeToo movement? An article in the *Guardian* seems to suggest that it's a bit of a joke to consider the film a 'feminist comedy'. It claims that it 'bears the same relationship to feminism that *Jurassic Park* does to palaeontology'. Whoa there, opinion piece! Yes, the film *is* dated (although those glasses are making a comeback) and, yes, perhaps some of the lines are not the most savoury now, but as film journalist Nikki Baughan argues in her article for the BFI, if the central idea is looked at closely while ignoring the Eighties paraphernalia, the film can be seen as 'a socialist feminist fantasy, a rousing exploration of the potentially transformative power of sisterhood, solidarity and unashamed, unrestricted ambition'. And although the boss is almost cartoonish in his portrayal, it shows how the *man* can act appallingly and *still* get promoted above much more capable and qualified women. An Eighties big-budget Hollywood film was never going to be a perfect representation of the feminist movement, so why do we insist that every part of a film has to be on message to make it a powerful and worthwhile endeavour? It is thoroughly entertaining, but it manages to cleverly squeeze some really important messages in there, too. Many of us still dream of an on-site crèche facility and equal pay, do we not? And this was adopted in a film made 40 years ago!

So, we can say that *9 to 5* undoubtedly highlighted some of the issues that the #MeToo movement has tackled head-on several decades later, particularly the way the patriarchy blocks attempts to achieve equality, and the sense of entitlement and perceived ownership abusers often have over victims' bodies. Even though *9 to 5* is 40 years old, it is still relevant today, which is no doubt why

'IT COT A LOT OF MONEY TO LOOK THI$ CHEAP'

there's a sequel with the original cast and producers in the works! Dolly's character has a lot of parallels with how people perceive her in real life. She has been consistently called a 'dumb blonde', with many people underestimating her because of her typically 'feminine' and glamorous looks, but this has not limited her in any way. Remember, when you assume, you make an *ass* out of *u* and *me*! And who is laughing all the way to the success bank? That's right, Queen Dolly. When you think about it, it is truly mad to judge someone's ability to be successful by their bodies, the colour of their hair and the length of their hemline!

BE MORE DOLLY

☆

If a person's behaviour is making you feel uncomfortable, tell someone. Doralee found help through her sisters!

☆

How you look – and want to look – is no one else's business but yours. Looking different to how people think you 'should' look does not mean you're not capable or worthy. Wear whatever you want to!

☆

Never underestimate someone. It is cruel and will come to bite you in your denimed ass!

Some might say that Dolly's style is *uhm* trashy … but, you know what? That is *exactly* what she wants it to be. As a young girl growing up in difficult financial circumstances, you can see where this slightly over-the-top, super-glamorous look came from and why it might have appealed to tiny Dolly. She retells the story of when she found her style muse: 'There was this one woman, I thought she was beautiful and, you know, she had the peroxide hair and she had it all piled up on her head and had red fingernails and red lipstick and, you know, wore her powder. And I just thought she was the prettiest thing I'd ever seen. And Mama said, "Oh, quit looking at her. She ain't nothing but trash." And I thought, "Ooh, that's what I want to be when I grow up – trash."'

Dolly has never been one to be concerned with what fashion tells her to wear, swinging from full denim outfits in the Seventies to bedazzled catsuits in the Eighties. Her hair is her crowning glory and as she likes to joke: 'People always ask me how long it takes me to do my hair. I don't know, I'm never there!' Her wig collection is legendary. Dolly reminds us that we don't need to take ourselves too seriously and that our outward appearance is just one side of our personality. You want to go to the shops in a full rhinestone outfit? You do that! You want to wear a wig to the dentist to give yourself an extra confidence boost? Why not? You want your nails to be on point for gardening? Go for it! But equally, you don't want to wear make-up every day? You don't want to dye your hair? You do you!

Although Dolly is releasing a clothing and jewellery line that is set to bring her 'iconic style and personality to her millions of fans worldwide', we get that her look isn't for everyone, because not everyone is Dolly! You have to figure out what works for you.

Recreating her style isn't what we should focus on; it's learning to adopt the way clothes make her *feel* that's important. Adopting her positive attitude and indifference to others' opinions is the most useful takeaway. *This* is what we should try to emulate.

Dolly's look also reflects her strong values and morals. Why should she change because fashion changes and other people's tastes move on? Staying true to what she believes is right for her and *not* being influenced by external factors is another part of what makes up the wonderful Dollyverse. If we try to embody just *one* thing from Dolly, it should be her unflinching belief in herself and what she is doing.

BE MORE DOLLY

☆

Have you worked out what you feel comfortable in? If not, try out some new looks and see how each one makes you feel. Do you feel more confident or self-conscious? If you are spending all your time worrying about how you look, or how other people are thinking you look, you won't have time to focus on the important stuff.

☆

If you want to follow fashion trends, go for it! Remember that just because something is fashionable doesn't necessarily mean it is comfortable for you, so think before you buy the next exciting new thing. Ask yourself why you're buying it. Is it because you like it and will wear it a lot, or is it because everyone else is wearing it?

> ☆
>
> *If you don't want to be judged by how you look or what you are wearing, don't judge others either. You don't know what has influenced them and why they look the way they do, so just be kind.*
>
> ☆
>
> *To be like someone, you don't have to look like them. You should find your own way and your own trademark style. Then you'll feel more confident and be bossing it in no time!*

How to be an icon the Dolly way:

- Find your style and stay true to it. Is it something that inspires you? Is it something you find comfortable or practical? Whatever it is, enjoy it.

- Look out for each other as the trio in 9 to 5 did! Friends are there to support each other, so make sure you have each other's backs.

- Don't put up with unacceptable behaviour just because 'things have always been that way'. If it doesn't feel right and you don't feel comfortable, it's probably because it isn't right. Confide in those friends of yours and talk to them about what you should do.

- Go and watch 9 to 5 again – maybe grab some friends to watch it with. It is pure Eighties gold and the hair, make-up and outfits are to die for. You'll be smiling and singing in no time!

'You always want your people to be proud of what you have accomplished.'

From Sevier County to Hollywood, to Dollywood. Dollywood opened its salon doors in 1986. The theme park was previously known as Goldrush Junction and Silver Dollar City, but the year it opened as Dollywood saw its numbers double. For those who haven't been, or those who just want to relive it in all its glory, let's take a moment to appreciate some of the amazing attractions at Dollywood. There's the Dollywood Express, which is a real-life coal-fired steam train that takes you on a five-mile journey around the Smoky Mountains. There's also the one-room wooden chapel that is named after the doctor who delivered Dolly, Robert F. Thomas. There is an exact replica of Dolly's childhood home – a two-room wooden house that didn't have electricity or running water – where you can step back in time on a tour. There are, of course, dinner shows, too, to keep you entertained, such as 'Dolly Parton's Stampede', which includes 32 horses and their riders doing tricks such as jumping through huge hoops of fire, and also 'Pirates Voyage', which is an acrobatic spectacle with *actual* mermaids (they're real) in the 'sea' around the giant pirate ship, all while you eat a good ol' southern meal. Other shows include 'My People, My Music', which has Dolly's brother Randy and other family members singing about their family and home in the mountains. There is even a hologram of Dolly in the Chasing Rainbows Museum!

'I just love what I do. I never outgrew my childhood and my family and my people ... that keeps me anchored, that keeps me grounded. I'm just doing what I've always wanted to do, what I dreamed of doing, so it makes me happy.'

Dolly Parton's Mountain Home

Dollywood is now the biggest employer in Pigeon Forge and the most ticketed attraction in Tennessee. It is another business adventure that has had the Dolly rhinestone touch! But why would Dolly invest in a theme park in her home county? Well, it's because of the love she has for her community. In an interview in 2010 she said, 'I always thought that if I made it big or got successful at what I had started out to do, that I wanted to come back to my part of the country and do something great, something that would bring in a lot of jobs into this area.' Dollywood is not the only investment Dolly has made in Sevier County. The hospital owes a lot to Dolly's desire to help the community. There are two departments named after her: the Dolly Parton Birthing Unit and the Dolly Parton Center for Women's Services.

Now, don't worry if you can't afford to even install a swing in your local park, let alone open a theme park; just let Dolly inspire you to become part of your community! There are so many good reasons to dive right in and make connections where you can. According to Johann Hari in his book *Lost Connections*, there are nine causes of depression, seven of which are from different types of disconnection, including: 'from other people, from meaningful values and from a future that makes sense to you'.

Dolly has decided to stay connected to her past and her people to help create a wonderful future for herself and those around her. By creating more jobs in her home county, she has ensured that more people can stay there rather than having to move away for work, so they can stay connected to their people and their roots. Their future is not decided for them just because they happened to be born in a certain place or at a certain time. It also means the

area is not 'dying'; as job prospects improve, young people will be more likely to stay there, meaning young families can flourish and bring vitality to the county.

We're all aware that loneliness has been cited as a global modern epidemic. Health insurance company Cigna found that nearly half of all Americans admit to feeling lonely. This study was cross-generational, with young people coming out on top as the most likely to say they feel lonely. One of the reasons stated for this is the lack of a regular workplace in the 'gig economy'. Interestingly, the study suggests that the start of loneliness can be traced back to the Industrial Revolution when closely-connected agricultural communities were broken apart when they were forced to move away for work. Dollywood gives its employees a sense of belonging, so they don't need to leave their hometown for work and can stay connected to their loved ones.

'I didn't leave here
to get away from my people.
I wanted to see the world,
but I was always proud
to be a country girl.'

Dolly understands the importance of friends. Judy Ogle has been Dolly's best friend for over 60 years. Having met as little children, they then reunited in Nashville later in their lives and have been by each other's side ever since. As well as keeping Dolly rooted in her humble beginnings, Judy offers all the physical and mental benefits that having a close friend brings – benefits that are slowly being recognised.

A study by the University of Michigan showed that when women feel close and comfortable with a friend, it increases the hormone progesterone, which in turn reduces feelings of anxiety and stress. Dolly has a very busy and stressful job, so having her good friends close by at all times must undoubtedly help her to mellow. We all know how helpful it is to air our grievances or share our joy with a close friend!

An Australian Longitudinal Study of Ageing recently found that closer connections with friends can have a positive impact on your health and lifespan. They found that close connections with friends was of more benefit to you than relationships with your children or other family members. However, it is the *quality* of the friendships that count as there is little benefit to superficial connections. We all knew that hanging out with our most trusted pals made us feel loved and cared for! After all, who else would put up with our Dolly obsession?

BE MORE DOLLY

☆

Who is your closest and most trusted friend?
Factor in some time to see them regularly. Remember,
a good old chinwag may have the same effect as a yoga
class (well, you might feel a reduction in stress.
Not sure you'll be any more bendy afterwards).

☆

Are there any local activities or events you could attend that
will make you feel more a part of your local community?

☆

Make a list below of your closest circle of friends and
make a note of how they make you feel.

....

....

....

....

....

....

Dolly doesn't just have love for us humans; she is a dog lover, too (aren't all the best people?)! After her performance at Glastonbury in 2014, a dog was found abandoned in a tent. The poor pup was named after Dolly because her performance had just pulled in the biggest-ever crowd at the festival. She took to Twitter to say that she'd take the doggy Dolly if no one was to claim her. Dolly even reportedly had her management call the rescue centre where doggy Dolly was being cared for, to make sure she was being looked after properly. Could she be any more perfect?

Did you know that Dolly is such a fan of dogs that she even immortalised a childhood dog in the song 'Cracker Jack'? Have a listen, but if you're feeling slightly fragile save it for another day, because it'll spark tears galore!

Dolly understands the benefits that having a dog can bring to our lives. She knows that Mr Foof the Pomeranian is not going to allow you to stay in bed all day in a pit of self-pity; he is going to get you out and about in the beautiful sunshine (or rain) and breathing fresh air (depending on where you are). Dolly also knows that having a pooch makes us more sociable. Just imagine that you're pottering along with Dolly the dachshund and who do you bump into? Mr Jackson from down the road walking his old Jack Russell Dodger and … boom! You're making connections in the community, which gives you a sense of belonging, and, you never know, might just have brightened Mr Jackson's day, too. Then Dolly and Dodger can become best friends, and it's win, win!

Dolly also understands that having a dog lowers stress. The physical act of stroking a pet relaxes you, but the general companionship and long walks in the countryside also help to lower

stress levels. Dogs are a wonderful antidote to loneliness and their need for daily routine and lots of care brings structure and meaning to everyday life.

Dolly talks about how her dog Popeye (great name) the Boston terrier helped her through a very dark time. She recognises how loving and caring dogs can be, and even let the animal rights charity PETA use her song 'Will He Be Waiting for Me' in an ad campaign, reminding people that dogs need company and can't be left alone. Dolly and dogs are a dream combination!

How to love your community the Dolly way:

- Friends are super important. Make sure you find the time to see them, even if it is just once a week. You'll notice the difference straight away and feel more relaxed in no time.
- What small thing could you do for your community? Any small deed will help! Make a list of ideas below and maybe see if there's something you could do with a friend. It is always easier to do things with a friend, as it encourages and motivates you. It also means you are more likely to stick to it, too!
- Remember, people are all we have, so look out for each other!

....

....

....

'You've gotta be great friends. And you've gotta be able to be accepting and just kind of know that you're not gonna change that person, because you married him because you loved 'em for what they were.'

Dolly and her husband Carl Dean celebrated their fiftieth wedding anniversary in 2016 by renewing their vows in a private ceremony in Nashville. This is an amazing feat for anyone, but it's particularly huge for a Hollywood celebrity, as we all know most celebs' marriages are lucky to last five months, let alone 50 years!

Dolly herself has revealed that the secret to their long marriage is … time apart. With Dolly's crazy schedule, they spend a great deal of time away from each other, but this means they really do enjoy the time they spend together. According to an article in *Psychology Today*, spending time apart doing what you enjoy and then spending quality time together is a mark of a very healthy relationship.

Carl is rarely seen out and about with Dolly and is an intensely private person. From the outside, he seems completely different to Dolly, but do you want to know why it works? It's because Dolly respects that Carl wants different things but supports her in everything she does. Respecting one another's differences is crucial, even if you disagree on important matters. Carl set his boundaries early on in the relationship. He was open about not wanting to go to high-profile events. Dolly recounts the time Carl turned to her after attending an awards ceremony in 1966 and said: 'Dolly, I want you to have everything you want, and I'm happy for you, but don't you ever ask me to go to another one of them dang things again!'

'I'll never harden my heart, but I've toughened the muscles around it.'

Setting boundaries is one of the most important aspects of a fulfilling relationship. Journalist Jennifer Twardowski in an article for *Huffpost* states simply that 'boundaries are what set the space between where you end and the other person begins'. Just because Carl doesn't like flashy events doesn't mean he is going to stop Dolly going to them. They respect each other and that's what makes their relationship a healthy one – no ghosting here!

Dolly knows that being in a long-term relationship doesn't suit everybody, and that some people just prefer their own space. All she cares about is that her fans are happy and content. Being single can be incredible. It gives you the chance to really discover what you want and what you like outside of being in a couple. It makes you realise what is important to you and what is important to have in a partner (if you want one!). You can go anywhere and do anything without having to check in with anyone – it's true freedom. You have time to work on hobbies and hang out with friends. Al! of your free time is *your* time and you get to decide how to spend that precious energy. When and if you meet someone and decide to share that energy and time with them, you will know it is because you want to and because that person is worth it.

There is no denying that being in a relationship requires a certain amount of work. You are no longer just thinking about yourself and what you want, you have to constantly consider another person. But having support and kindness around you can give you the safety and room in your brain to focus on finding your version of success. According to relationship counsellor Stan Tatkin, if you're in a supportive relationship, you have the energy and time to work towards being successful rather than worrying and stressing about your other half. He also stresses even if couples marry and have kids, they should always see each other as they did in the earlier stages of the relationship. Love doesn't have to fizzle out or become practical if you make time to have dates, do kind things for each other and gaze lovingly into each other's eyes.

However, if you find yourself with somebody who at times makes you feel uneasy, uncertain or insecure, Dolly would tell you to get the hell out of there and find what you're truly looking for. Dolly is walking proof that only a happy, *committed* relationship will bring you contentment and creativity.

BE MORE DOLLY

If you're in a long-term relationship, think about the last time you did something by yourself, for yourself. A long time ago, eh? Put some time in the diary to do something you enjoy.

☆

When your partner is being annoying, remember that everyone is annoying – sometimes even you are annoying – so be kind and try to focus on their good qualities.

Do you and your partner still enjoy date nights? Sitting in your threadbare PJs watching Netflix and eating mac and cheese doesn't really count (although please invite us round next time you do this as we love that). When was the last time you did something fun together just for the hell of it? Well, grab that diary again and plan some fun activities! They don't have to be fancy or expensive, they just have to be different from your normal day-to-day routines. Remember, you should never stop dating and getting to know each other. It is so important to keep the energy and excitement in a relationship and not take each other for granted.

If you're not in a long-term relationship, think about if you have clear boundaries in your relationships with others. Remember, it's OK to say what you want!

Even though Dolly has been in a committed relationship for over half a century, she sure does know how to write a song or two about love and heartache. Talking about her passion for writing about love in an interview with *Vice* in 2016, she said:

'I'm a hopeless romantic … I got my fantasies, but I write for everybody else that can't write their feelings; so many of the songs on the record are based on other people's relationships, people

I care about that don't know how to write it, but of course I've felt all those feelings. I'm married, but I ain't dead!'

Part of Dolly's great appeal is that her songs are super relatable and make us feel like she is right there with us. In an article in *Vice*, psychotherapist Mark O'Connell says that listening to songs about love and loss lets us experience collective heartbreak in a safe and contained way. In the same article, psychotherapist Abigail Burd explains that by listening to these sorts of songs it helps you understand that this is a common human experience and it will get better. An amazing songwriter like Dolly can express these complex human emotions a lot better than us mere mortals, and she shares this with us to help us all connect. One of the most inspiring songs is 'The Bargain Store', which is meant to remind people that even though it feels as though you have lots of baggage, you can come through things and find love again. As the quote at the beginning of this chapter states, Dolly will not harden her heart even if there have been tough times, as she knows the importance of love. Instead, she has worked on becoming resilient in the face of adversity.

As another Dolly once said (journalist Dolly Alderton, to be exact), it takes a village to mend a broken heart and Dolly Parton is a huge contributing member of that village. We might go so far as to say that she is the chief of said village.

BE MORE DOLLY

Which lyrics from Dolly's songs resonate with you the most?
Write them down and try to pinpoint why they mean so
much to you. Maybe get creative and decorate them to
go on your mirror so you can see them every day and give
yourself a nice boost!

Make a playlist of the most relatable Dolly songs to play
as and when you need a Dolly hug! Going through the
experience with someone else will make it easier and
eventually less painful.

Remember, it takes a village to mend a broken heart, so
surround yourself with friends, family and Dolly!

....

....

....

How to cope with love and heartache the Dolly way:

- Make time to do something you enjoy so that you have something outside of your relationship that is just for you.
- If you're in a long-term relationship, put regular date nights in the diary. Remember, it is important to have quality time together, not just time when you are doing the laundry or food shopping. Act as if you are still in the early stages of a relationship.
- Find solace in music, books, poems. Sometimes they just express your feelings so much better than you can yourself and it reminds you that everyone goes through tough times and they come out the other side.
- Also, remember that you are loved and you are special. Dolly knows it and we know it!

'I always just thought if you see somebody without a smile, give 'em yours!'

How many global megastars can say they have given away over 100 million free books to children across three continents? In February 2018, Dolly's Imagination Library initiative gave out its 100-millionth book. The initiative sends out a free book once a month to children aged 0–5 to encourage a love of reading.

Like her business acumen, Dolly's idea for the Imagination Library was inspired by her father (he sounds like a guy we should all have had in our lives!). Robert Lee Parton couldn't read or write, and she wanted to make sure that other people were not held back from learning these fundamental skills because of financial or other difficulties. Therefore, in 1996, the Imagination Library was born in Dolly's home county.

'The first step is always the hardest, but you'll never know unless you try ...'

And what steps Dolly has taken with this amazing charity! The programme went US-wide in 2000, then into Canada in 2006, over to the UK's shores in 2007 and then down under to Australia in 2013. It has won awards including the Best Practices Award from the Library of Congress Literacy in recognition of the huge amount of work the charity has done to promote literacy and reading. The charity has also recognised the need to make literacy as inclusive as possible and has therefore included audiobooks and Braille. In 2015 they brought in 12 bilingual titles in Spanish for the US and in 2018 the charity worked closely with the Assembly of First Nations in Canada to make sure that First Nations children had access to the programme.

The Dollywood Foundation, which originally implemented the Imagination Library, started in the early Nineties with Queen Dolly pledging $500 to every seventh- and eighth-grade student who finished high school in her county. This dramatically decreased the high-school dropout percentage! Every year the Foundation gives out five $15,000 scholarships to high-school graduates in Dolly's county for them to continue their education. All they have to do to receive this generous donation is communicate their dream and show how committed they are to it. (Doesn't this remind you of a young Dolly?)

And as if that wasn't enough of Dolly's philanthropic antics, when wild fires destroyed homes in her home county in 2016, the Foundation created the My People Fund, which helped distribute $1,000 every month for six months to every family whose home had been destroyed.

As well as helping us human folk, Dolly opened the Eagle Mountain Sanctuary in Dollywood in 1991. This houses the largest collection of bald eagles that can no longer live their free eagle life due to health problems which leave them unable to survive in the wild. Some of the eagles have had to have wing amputations due to their injuries, but they are diligently cared for by the staff at Dollywood.

In 2019, Dolly was awarded the title of MusiCares Person of the Year. She is the first ever country music star to win the award, so it's a fantastic achievement. MusiCares is a charity that provides support for people in the music industry when life gets hard. Dolly was recognised as Person of the Year due to her amazing charity work and all her incredible business and creative achievements. The announcement was made during the glamorous Grammy week's gala and tribute ceremony, all proceeds from which go to MusiCares.

Although not all of us can win an award for being the most philanthropic person ever, there are some other fantastic benefits to be found through volunteering. Researchers Eric Kim and Sara Konrath found that people over the age of 50 who volunteer spend 38 per cent fewer nights in hospital than those who don't. Another study looked at teenagers who volunteer and found that those who do are fitter than those who don't. This is great, right? If we all volunteer, we will be healthier, the world will be a better place … But there is a *slight* catch. The research shows that you have to *want* to do the volunteering for altruistic reasons, not just for your own personal welfare. You have got to have a passion for what you're volunteering for and a real drive to want to do it. Otherwise your health stats are not that much better than those of people who aren't volunteering. According to Eric Kim, the real reason you are getting healthier when volunteering is because you are meeting the need for a purpose in life. If you are just going through the motions, you are not meeting that need. However, every person should be able to find a cause they care enough about to want to help, and if that's the case then we might be on to a winner with volunteering as a health boost.

BE MORE DOLLY

Is there a cause you are passionate about? Is there a way you could volunteer for it, even in a small way? Make a list of possible charities/causes you could support.

Volunteering is not just great for the charity, it is a way for you to meet new people and maybe obtain new skills. Want to learn about wildlife but can't afford the time or money to go back to school? Volunteer with a wildlife charity in your spare time instead. That way, everyone's a winner! It will also give more meaning to your life if you find you are not getting that from your paid work.

Dolly knows people are not an island; everyone needs help and support at one time in their life. Think how you could become part of a community, rather than just chasing the rat race.

Giving back is not just about charitable donations or volunteering, it's also about forgiveness. Dolly is a great proponent of forgiveness. One story that really demonstrates this involves her ex-TV partner, Porter Wagoner. Dolly had decided it was time for her to leave Wagoner's long-running syndicated country show and break out on her own when she was becoming more and more successful as a solo artist and wanted to spread her wings. However, Wagoner had a slightly different idea. Even though Dolly had written her incredible

single 'I Will Always Love You' to show him that she needed to leave (and he had seemed to accept this), he tried to sue Dolly for $3 million in lost potential earnings. She ended up paying him $1 million. As well as all the suing, he wasn't particularly kind about Dolly in the press afterwards. However, when Wagoner fell on hard times later in his career and Dolly was forging ahead, she made the decision to buy the publishing rights to his songs and give them back to him for free. This was an astonishing act of forgiveness. Dolly had become much more successful than Wagoner, and could have seen his downturn as comeuppance for his earlier behaviour towards her, but she realised that he was hurting when he hurt her, and if she could help him in any way, she would.

Just like in the song 'I Will Always Love You', she wished him only good things. Therefore, Dolly really does practise what she preaches. Like the rest of us, she lives by the sentiments in her songs. Dolly understands how important forgiveness is. It helps us to dissipate anger and resentment, because what does bearing a grudge actually achieve in the long run? Forgiveness doesn't mean you are accepting the behaviour of the person who has hurt or upset you or that you are automatically reconciling with them. Someone 'wronging' you, however, shouldn't always discount their previous loving and caring behaviour. It's good to take a step back and review the incident in context. If somebody hurts you and, as a result, you decide you want them out of your life, that's absolutely fine. What you shouldn't do is dwell on the bad ending and use up your energy being angry and resentful. It will hinder the healing process.

Sometimes you may have a strong sense of justice – that people should pay for their mistakes – but it's helpful to remind yourself that it's not really your job to make that happen. Focus on the positive aspects of the time you spent with that person, what you learnt, what you gained. If they have truly hurt and upset you, they will be paying for that for a long time by themselves. Remember, hurt doesn't necessarily have to beget hurt. Rage and resentment can feel like a 50-ton weight on your shoulders and will unknowingly seep into everything you say and do. The release that forgiveness can bring will allow you to create more space to think and focus on things like creativity, love, joy – you know, the good stuff.

It is also really important to be able to forgive yourself. You may not even be aware that you are holding on to unresolved anger. As we've already said, people make mistakes, everyone is annoying, most people are just trying to do their best with the resources and education they grew up with, with the finances available to them and the emotional support they've been given. It might sometimes feel like everyone is out to get you, but on the whole they're really not. People are too ready to blame each other, but a blame culture doesn't move things forward, it just makes people fearful. No one wants to be the focus of blame, as it triggers shame and stunts progress. When we feel shame, we are backed into a corner and cannot be our best Dolly selves! In the world of work, you might notice a lot of blame culture, but remember that it will always be more useful to try to understand *why* people have made a mistake. Do they not have enough time to do the job properly? Have they not had the necessary training to get the job right? Have they got things going on outside of work that are causing distress? Are they not as engaged in the job as they should be? These are the factors that *should* be explored, but a lot of the time people want answers quickly, and the easiest thing to do is point the finger rather than fixing the source of the problem. If you find yourself in this situation, just think, 'What would Dolly do?' and the answer should become clear …

BE MORE DOLLY

☆

Be open to the idea of forgiveness. This can be complicated and not easy to do, but even a bit of self-exploration will open up your mind to the possibility of it. Remember that forgiveness does not mean you're being a doormat!

☆

Think about how much more space you'll have in your life for positive and lovely things if you are able to let go of anger and resentment.

How to give back the Dolly way:

- Give back to yourself, as well as others. You cannot pour from an empty cup, so make sure that you look after yourself and then you will be better equipped to look after others.

- Forgiveness is not weakness; in fact, it is courage and strength. The ability to forgive will make people respect you, but more importantly, it will make you respect yourself!

- Volunteer whatever you can, be it time, money, your skills or even just your smile. We're all in this world together and have to live with each other, so let's make it a nicer place to be.

'If you talk bad things about country music, it's like saying bad things about my momma. Them's fightin' words.'

Got a dilemma you can't solve? Feeling a bit blue or out of sorts? Here is the bible of Dolly songs to meet your soul's needs.

Feeling a bit insecure and need a boost? Your song is:

- **'THE BARGAIN STORE'**
  Dolly reassures you that everyone has been through tough times, but you're human and we're all in this together. Parts of you might be a bit broken and dusty, but if you get the affection, love and attention you deserve, you'll be right as rain and ready to love again! The strolling bassline on this song will have you hooking your thumbs in your belt hooks and grapevining in no time, maybe with a knee slap or two – oh, and an obligatory tip of your hat.

When the daily grind is getting you down:

- **'9 TO 5'**
  What else could it be? Everyone knows the pain of a Monday-morning rush hour, but you got this! Did you know that the

amazing typewriter beat at the start of the song was crafted by Dolly on the set by strumming her nails together? Genius! Also, if you really need that extra boost, we beg you to watch the official music video. The mullets are pure heaven and we're not sure what clipboard man's game is in the background – maybe drop us a line if you figure out what his role is!

When you feel like getting emosh with a friend or loved one:

- **'ISLANDS IN THE STREAM'**
  Grab that hairbrush or Prosecco bottle and sing this with your bestie! A classic duet for the ages, but did you know it was written by the Bee Gees and that the title was taken from an Ernest Hemingway novel? Which shows that this little duet has a lot of depth to it and should be taken seriously.

When you need to feel some love or want to show someone how you feel:

- **'HERE I AM'**
  Originally released by Dolly in 1971, it has been rereleased as a duet with Sia for the Netflix movie *Dumplin'*. Get ready to feel some feels! This song has a massive dollop of soul in it and feels like a mix of gospel anthem and Seventies guitar jam. Dolly's voice in the new rendition is so raw and full of emotion. Sometimes she just says things so much better than anyone else can, and this is one of those times.

When those Tinder dates are going hideously and the ghosting is real, just remember, you're not the only one:

- **'HOLDIN' ON TO YOU'**

  Dolly knew the struggle was real even in 1977. How often do we hold on too long to that 'perfect' person even when they treat us badly? Well, Dolly knows this truth, too! Why won't you take up with the person who wants to make you happy and help you get to the places you want to go? Because you're human and it bloomin' well happens to all of us, but maybe one day you'll realise that you deserve that amazing person after all.

When the patriarchy has really got you down:

- **'JUST BECAUSE I'M A WOMAN'**

  This song has so many truth bombs in it, it hurts. Please just listen to it. This is classic country: the slow clop that sounds like cowboys sauntering into town on horseback; the lyrical strings; the emotional lilt of Dolly's voice overlaying it all. This will make you want to sit down on a bale of hay, strum on a guitar and stare pensively into the distance in search of the one that got away.

When you need a morning anthem:

- **'BETTER GET TO LIVIN''**

  This summarises all of Dolly's life advice in an upbeat jingle. Your colleagues will be confused as to why you're so jolly if you listen to this on the way to the office! The video for this song is deeply,

deeply odd. But we do now have our next Halloween costume sorted: Dolly as a ringmaster in a circus … amazing!

When you want to slow dance:

'OLD FLAMES (CAN'T HOLD A CANDLE TO YOU)'
This feels like ultimate Dolly. Slow country guitar with her smooth dulcet tones laying luxuriously over the top. You can whisper in the ear of your loved one as you're dancing that even though you've had many lovers (hey, we're not judging!), none of them could hold a candle to the one you're with now … Awww …

When you know it is time to move on:

- ### 'IT'S TOO LATE'
  This is a brilliant song for reminding yourself why you needed to let that person go. It will keep your strength and resolve going. Do not let that person back in! Dolly just makes it so painfully clear: they are too late, they made their decision, now it is time for you to move on and find the person you deserve.

When you spy your ex's new partner online:

- ### 'I HOPE YOU'RE NEVER HAPPY'
  This starts off with Dolly wishing the person all the happiness in the world and you question whether you read the title right, but then she serves a curveball. She only wishes all of these wonderful things if the person stays with her! Legend. Isn't this

what you think every time you see your ex-partner with someone new? Even if it ended amicably and smelling of roses, you know deep down you wish them misery for ever. How dare they think they could be as happy with someone else as they were with you! Because, in all seriousness, you were the best thing that ever happened to them and they will live to regret the day they thought they knew better.

When you let that questionable person back in your life:

- **'HERE YOU COME AGAIN'**
  The one person you promised your friends you would never get back with, and, more importantly, promised yourself you would never go near again, has slid back into your DMs and you can't help but smile. Well, Dolly understands your predicament. But maybe knowing that even the great Dolly can go through this might help you ignore their 'Hey, stranger, long time no speak' message.

When anyone judges you on how you look:

- **'BACKWOODS BARBIE'**
  When people ask you why you love Dolly Parton so much, or question her talent because of how she looks, or query whether or not she is a good role model, you just play them this song. This explains everything they need to know about Dolly and why she looks the way she does and why that shouldn't matter one jot. This will make you feel warm to your toes and will hopefully

make you gentler on yourself and others. We are all guilty of judging a book by its cover!

When you're feeling randy:

- **'BABY I'M BURNIN''**
  When we say 'randy' we mean you're six tequilas into the first night you've had out for months and your lifelong love is busting some serious moves on the dance floor and you don't know why you haven't jumped their bones already. This is the song you need. It has some serious Seventies disco vibes and even some amazing keyboard laser sound effects. (You know the ones we mean – the ones you used in your school music class to show people how talented and creative you were. Don't worry, they will never understand your talent, but Dolly does.)

When you are feeling nostalgic and maybe a little homesick:

- **'MY TENNESSEE MOUNTAIN HOME'**
  Basically, the state anthem for Tennessee. Even if you didn't grow up in the Smoky Mountains, this song will inspire that wonderful feeling of longing for home and the innocence of childhood. The sense of place it evokes reminds you of long summers with family and childhood friends, the balmy air and smell of hot earth. It'll make you want to sling your arms around your loved ones and sway from side to side as you belt out the chorus with all your heart.

And then, for every other occasion:

- 'JOLENE'

  Maybe your loved one is pining after a beautiful redhead – hey, it happens! – or maybe you just need to bellow out the catchiest, most beautiful tune ever …

Badass Singin' Septuagenarians

As we've already seen, age ain't nothing but a number for our Dolly, but she is not the only one who has rocked it through the ages. Here's a list of some other inspiring musical legends.

Cher

The vocal powerhouse that is Cher was born the same year as Dolly. She recently performed her second 82-show farewell tour 'Here We Go Again' across America, Europe and Australasia. Cher, like Dolly, is also an actress, receiving an Oscar in 1988 for her role in *Moonstruck* and recently returning to the big screen in the iconic *Mamma Mia! Here We Go Again*. Dolly and Cher appeared together in a duet on a Cher TV special in 1978 called the 'Heaven and Hell Medley', in which Dolly was on the side of heaven trying to save Cher's soul and a band called The Tubes tried to tempt Cher to hell. We're not going to lie – the whole thing is sublimely odd. What else would we expect from a Seventies Dolly/Cher mash-up?

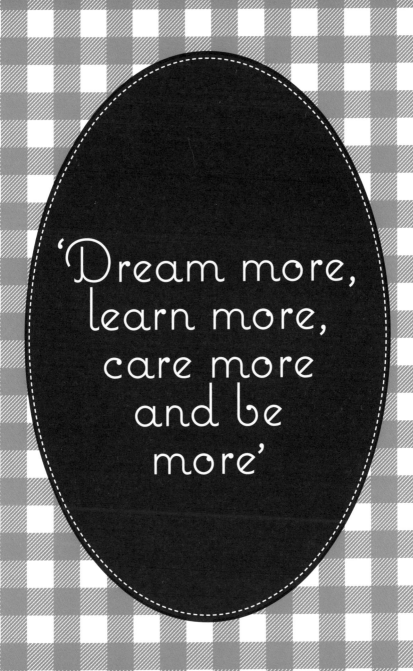

'Dream more,
learn more,
care more
and be
more'

Liza Minnelli

The four-time Tony Award winner, Oscar winner, two-time Golden Globe winner and Emmy winner was also born in the golden year of 1946. Liza is still touring on and off and teaching masterclasses at The Actor's Studio. Her résumé is pretty darn impressive and so is her family, as she is the daughter of American celebrity royalty Judy Garland and Vincente Minnelli. If you haven't seen *Cabaret* then this should be on your watchlist for this weekend!

Patti Smith

On a slightly different tack, Patti Smith was also born in 1946. Known as 'punk's poet laureate', her debut album *Horses* cemented her status in the punk scene in 1975. Patti's most famous song, 'Because The Night', was co-written with Bruce Springsteen. Patti's latest memoir, *The Year of the Monkey*, was released in her seventy-third year. Doesn't that just make you realise you still have lots of time to do amazing things? What an inspiration!

Linda Ronstadt

She might be *seriously* underrated, but Linda Ronstadt was one of the most successful singers of the 1970s. She had 10 Top-10 singles and made over 30 studio albums. Ronstadt retired in 2009 and was diagnosed with Parkinson's in 2013; a musical biopic was released in 2019 called *Linda Ronstadt: The Sound of My Voice*, which tracks her career across the decades. And guess who makes a guest appearance? That's right, Dolly is there sharing her memories of the singer. Linda also recorded a cover of 'I Will Always Love You' in 1975!

If these examples of extraordinary women don't give you some inspiration, we don't know what else will. To think, after five decades in the tough, gruelling and unforgiving entertainment industry they still have the get-up-and-go to continue to produce creative material and perform to sell-out crowds … It's a struggle to even fit all the Netflix in that we want to at our age, let alone write a new book or carry out an 82-date tour with full choreography (Cher, you are a goddess!). If only we could bottle what these guys have.

BE MORE LIKE DOLLY'S FRIENDS

☆

Reading about inspiring people's careers can sometimes give you the boost you need. Maybe pick a different successful person each week and see how their career has expanded and changed over the years. Remember that life isn't a sprint, it's a marathon, and looking at how people may have failed and succeeded is a reminder that you can do this.

☆

Talk to someone from a different generation – you never know what you might learn. Even though you might have very different opinions on some topics it's great to get a different perspective on things.

'It's hard to be
a diamond
in a rhinestone
world.'

How Dolly are you?

1. How many wigs do you own?

    a. I've got one I used for Halloween in 2001 that my cat currently uses as a bed.

    b. I would say a handful – you don't know when you're going to be called upon to be Wednesday Addams, Cher, Dolly (obviously) or Mrs Claus.

    c. The spare room is my wigdrobe.

2. How would you describe your fashion style?

    a. I'm pretty chilled – wearing a clean shirt is considered dressy for me.

    b. Smart casual, but I love to glam it up at the weekends and I wear the odd bejewelled cowboy boot on a Tuesday.

    c. I am glam de la glam and will wear what I want. Shopping in the supermarket in a rhinestone jumpsuit? I'm there!

3. What's your go-to karaoke song?

a. Oh God no, I don't sing!
b. I like to mix in a little Dolly and possibly Cher and Britney.
c. Only Dolly. Only Dolly.

4. What's your advice-giving style?

a. I don't feel I can give advice – it makes me anxious.
b. When the moment calls for it, but only if people ask!
c. I drop pearls of wisdom, left, right and centre. One of my own personal sayings is the background on my phone – do you want to see it?

5. What's your favourite instrument?

a. I'm not sure I have one. How can you tell the difference in a song?
b. I love the banjo.
c. I can't choose, but it would definitely be either the banjo or guitar or saxophone or piano …

6. What's your make-up routine like?

    a. Oh, I'm au naturel at all times.

    b. Love a false lash on a night out and a bold lip when the time calls for it.

    c. I won't step out of the house without the works. I've been known to take the hamster to the vets in full smoky eye.

7. How do you like to vacation?

    a. I'm all about the all-inclusive package holidays. No surprises or slumming it for me.

    b. I like to change it up every year. Maybe a glamping holiday one year, a beach one the next.

    c. Get me an RV and I'm ready to roll. Just me, my loved ones and the road. Oh yeah, and I like a little theme park every now and again.

Mostly As

Oooh, you're orbiting around the Dollyverse but have not sent out probes to really see if you would like it there! Start off easy, maybe listen to 'Jolene' a couple of hundred times and try watching *9 to 5* … you'll be hooked in no time.

Mostly Bs

Yes, you are dipping those rhinestoned cowboy-booted toes into the world of Dolly. To really step it up a bit we'd recommend attending the *9 to 5* musical and maybe planning a trip to Dollywood for the next family holiday. Soon.

Mostly Cs

Wow! Just wow! You are full-on Dolly and we salute you. People would have a hard time telling the two of you apart in a room (OK, maybe a dimly lit room), but, man, you have the Dolly *je ne sais quoi*! Go forth and spread the Dolly wisdom and way of life. We need more people like you in the world. Keep rockin'!

WHAT WOULD DOLLY DO?

Pick a scenario from the list below and then use Dolly's advice to try to solve that issue. Maybe you could add your own scenario below and see if any of the Dolly advice can help you work through it.

Scenario

You're nervous about taking up a new hobby – what if you're no good and everyone laughs at you?

You have to make a big decision at work and the advice your colleagues are giving you is just not helping …

You're just so busy, you feel like you're spinning a million different plates and you know something is going to fall and crash …

You're working on a project at work and you have a niggling feeling that it isn't going the way you planned …

Everything has gone wrong today: you were late for work, you forgot your lunch and to top it off, your partner/housemate forgot to tell you they weren't going to be home until late so you're eating alone again …

You have to go to a fancy event, but dressing up makes you feel really uncomfortable …

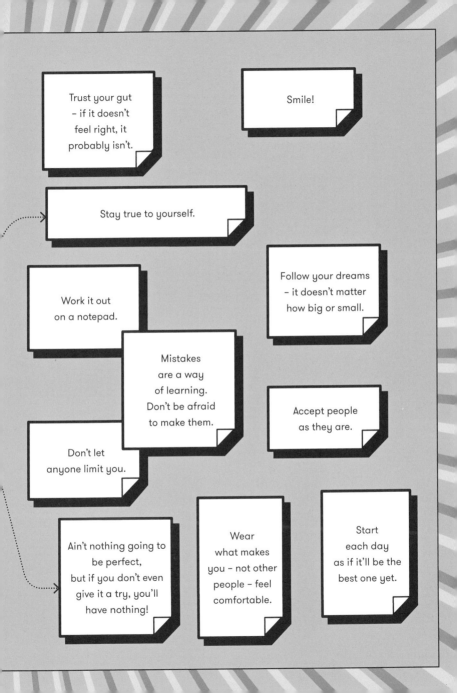

And We Will Always Love You, Dolly

So here we are. We've come through a lot over these hundred or so pages. We've learnt a lot more about Dolly and her incredible life over the past 70-odd years and we've learnt some things about ourselves, too. Being a Dolly fan means you're in a pretty cool club, so you're already taking a step in the right direction, but then learning some of her ultimate life lessons on top of that means you are now in the *super*-cool club. Welcome!

The essence of Dolly's wisdom, distilled down like some vintage southern whisky (the official state drink of Tennessee is milk, but that's not sexy, is it? You can't say Dolly's wisdom goes down a like glass of southern milk! Anyway, we digress …), is just be true to yourself, be kind and try to bring joy into this world. Man, that wisdom slips down nicely and leaves a warm afterglow, doesn't it? (Unlike milk, which leaves us cold and, if you're lactose intolerant, gassy.) We hope this little book has opened you up to new Dolly songs that you might not have experienced before and some new ideas for little changes that can make some big differences to how you feel day to day. We hope that you'll share some of these ideas with friends, family, dogs, cats and raccoons (official Tennessee state wild animal, official name: *Procyon lotor*, in case you were wondering), and that some of the advice will make you think about getting out there and making new connections, maybe starting a new hobby to keep that brain active. But we also hope this book encourages you not to take yourself too seriously – or anybody else for that matter.

'The way I see it,
if you want the rainbow,
you gotta put up with the rain.'

We thought we would leave you with one more Dolly quote to see you on your way. Life is full of rainbows, so do take the time to look out for them. They are pretty rare, so you'll have to put up with the storms life throws at you, and sometimes they will knock tiles off your roof, uproot trees and ruin an amazing hair day, but you only appreciate the good in life when you've experienced the bad. We need the bad to build resilience and to truly see what we can survive and make of ourselves. You have to do the work, though – people are there to support you, but if you don't have the drive and tenacity to do it, no one is going to do it for you.

Dolly's work ethic is infamous in the music business, but she always has a team of people around her. There was a quote doing the rounds for a while that said, 'You have the same number of hours in the day as Beyoncé' as a way to try to motivate people. It was another way of saying, 'Come on, Beyoncé does it all. Stop wasting your life watching TV and grouting your bathroom' – but it's so untrue. We do not have the same amount of time as Beyoncé as there isn't only one of her – she has a whole team running the machine, which makes that message completely unrealistic. It simply shames people into feeling like they are never doing enough. This quote from Dolly, however, is much more useful, because it encourages you to be kinder to yourself: 'Don't get so busy making a living that you forget to make a life.' You don't have to be achieving things 24/7, sometimes you can just be.

Rest is so important if you're to achieve everything you want. Although it looks as though Dolly is all about achieving and that she is 'on' all the time, she does actually take holidays and breaks. Burn-out is a very real phenomenon with very real consequences. There are many types of rest, too, not just sleep. It's OK to be unproductive sometimes. Nothing is a waste of time – it is all leading you towards where you need to be. Having little short breaks is a great idea – a change of scenery can do the world of good. Dolly and her husband reportedly go on long weekends in their camper just to get away and immerse themselves in nature. Deliberately scheduling in some downtime at home with no chores or responsibilities is so important. Head to an art gallery or a local park and just wander. Try not to listen to music or a podcast and just see if you can create a little space in your mind. Try to keep your phone away from you during your designated rest-time – it's all too easy to distract yourself, but if you do, you never really get to the good stuff – the part where your mind completely slows down and starts to relax. Give yourself permission to not always be 'on' and accessible for others; it is OK not to get back to that email/phone call/text message/social media message within five minutes, so don't punish yourself if you don't. If Dolly needed a break, Dolly would give herself a break. She hasn't made it this far in such a full-on industry without learning how to take a breather! And this is where we would like to leave you. It would be absolutely amazing if everyone could just be a bit more Dolly, but it would be equally great if everyone was just a bit more themselves. Once we are true to ourselves, we will be able to reach peak Dolly!

Parting Gift Inspiration

- Age ain't nothing but a number! If Dolly is still rocking it in her seventies, you can rock it, too!
- Dolly came from a two-room wooden cabin without running water or electricity to where she is today. Think about how far you could go.
- Dolly is a completely self-taught musician. Her 'try your hand at anything' mentality has got her far, so why don't you have a go?
- Dolly is proud of where she came from and has been instrumental in helping the area. This shows that you can always create good and beautiful things out of tough beginnings.
- Dolly has had setbacks in her long career, but she hasn't let them define her – she has just kept on going. So can you!
- Dolly has been misjudged many times because of her looks, but her strong resolve has meant she hasn't changed because of this. Stay strong and true to who you are.
- Dolly is an incredible businesswoman and she would've had to learn a lot of this herself in the early days, but she did it and she has nailed it!

BE MORE DOLLY

Resources & Further Reading

Booth, Jessica, 'Dolly Parton's Marriage: Things You Didn't Know' *The List*

Bryer, Tanya and Gibbs, Alexandra, 'Dolly Parton: The Time I Turned Down Elvis' *CNBC*, June 2016

Flippo, Chet, 'Interview: Dolly Parton' *Rolling Stone Magazine*, August 1977

Freeman, Hadley, 'Dolly Parton on Sexual Politics: "I've Probably Hit on Some People Myself!"' *Guardian*, February 2019

Friskics-Warren, Bill, 'The Other Dolly Parton, The Songwriting One' *New York Times*, July 2002

Hattenstone, Simon, 'I was Born with a Happy Heart' *Guardian*, May 2008

Hotson, Elizabeth, 'Dolly Parton's Nine-to-five Approach to Music' *bbc.co.uk*, October 2017

Lindsey, Michelle, 'Dolly Parton's Discography – The Bargain Store – Album Review' *Highway Queens*, November 2018

Kelly, Kim, 'Everyone Loves Dolly' *Vice*, September 2016

Schwabel, Dan, 'Dolly Parton: Her Personal Philosophy, Life Obstacles, and Best Advice' *Forbes* Magazine, November 2012

Severson, Kim, 'Dollywood: A Little Bit Country, a Little Bit Gay' *New York Times*, August 2017

Stych, Anne, 'Still Working 9 to 5: Dolly Parton Expands her Business Empire' *Biz Journals*, May 2019

https://imaginationlibrary.com/the-dollywood-foundation/